North American Indians Today

North American Indians Today

Apache

Cherokee

Cheyenne

Comanche

Creek

Crow

Huron

Iroquois

Navajo

Ojibwa

Osage

Potawatomi

Pueblo

Seminole

Sioux

North American
Indians Today

Cherokee

by
Philip Stewart

Mason Crest Publishers
Philadelphia

Mason Crest Publishers Inc.
370 Reed Road
Broomall, Pennsylvania 19008
(866) MCP-BOOK (toll free)

First printing
1 2 3 4 5 6 7 8 9 10
Library of Congress Cataloging-in-Publication Data on file at the Library of Congress.
ISBN: 1-59084-665-6
1-59084-663-X (series)

Design by Lori Holland.
Composition by Bytheway Publishing Services, Binghamton, New York.
Cover design by Benjamin Stewart.
Printed and bound in the Hashemite Kingdom of Jordan.

Photography by Benjamin Stewart. Pictures on pp. 6, 56, 77 by Keith Rosco. Photo on
p. 73 courtesy of Martha Berry; p. 78 courtesy of Brad Carson's office; p. 81 courtesy
of Viola Ruelke Gommer.
Cover: Robbie Jack/Corbis.

Contents

Why is it so important that Indians be brought into the "mainstream" of American life?
I would not know how to interpret this phrase to my people.
The closest I would be able to come would be "a big wide river".
Am I then to tell my people that they are to be thrown into the big, wide river of the United States?

Earl Old Person
Blackfeet Tribal Chairman

Introduction

In the midst of twenty-first–century North America, how do the very first North Americans hold on to their unique cultural identity? At the same time, how do they adjust to the real demands of the modern world? Earl Old Person's quote on the opposite page expresses the difficulty of achieving this balance. Even the common values of the rest of North America—like fitting into the "mainstream"—may seem strange or undesireable to North American Indians. How can these groups of people thrive and prosper in the twenty-first century without losing their traditions, the ways of thinking and living that have been handed down to them by their ancestors? How can they keep from drowning in North America's "big, wide river"?

Thoughts from the Series Consultant

Each of the books in this series was written with the help of Native scholars and tribal leaders from the particular tribe. Based on oral histories as well as written documents, these books describe the current strategies of each Native nation to develop its economy while maintaining strong ties with its culture. As a result, you may find that these books read far differently from other books about Native Americans.

Over the past centuries, Native groups have faced increasing pressure to conform to the wishes of the governments that took their lands. Often brutally inhumane methods were implemented to change Native social systems. These books describe the ways that Native groups refused to be passive recipients of change, even in the face of these past atrocities. Heroic individuals worked to fit external changes into local conditions. This struggle continues today.

The legacy of the past still haunts the psyche of both Native and non-Native people of North America; hopefully, these books will help correct some misunderstandings. And even with the difficulties encountered by past and current Native leaders, Native nations continue to thrive. As this series illustrates, Native populations continue to increase—and they have clearly persevered against incredible odds. North American culture's big, wide river may be deep and cold—but Native Americans are good swimmers!

—Martha McCollough

Breaking Stereotypes

One way that some North Americans may "drown" Native culture is by using stereotypes to think about North American Indians. When we use stereotypes to think about a group of people, we assume things about them because of their race or cultural group. Instead of taking time to understand individual differences and situations, we lump together everyone in a certain group. In reality, though, every person is different. More than two million Native people live in North America, and they are as *diverse* as any other group. Each one is unique.

Even if we try hard to avoid stereotypes, however, it isn't always easy to know what words to use. Should we call the people who are native to North America Native Americans—or American Indians—or just Indians?

The word "Indian" probably comes from a mistake—when Christopher Columbus arrived in the New World, he thought he had reached India, so he called the people he found there Indians. Some people feel it doesn't make much sense to call Native Americans "Indians." (Suppose Columbus had thought he landed in China instead of India; would we today call Native people "Chinese"?) Other scholars disagree; for example, Russell Means, Native politician and activist, claims that the word "Indian" comes from Columbus saying the native people were *en Dios*—"in God," or naturally spiritual.

Many Canadians use the term "First Nations" to refer to the Native peoples who live there, and people in the United States usually speak of Native Americans. Most Native people we talked to while we were writing these books prefer the simple term "Indian"—or they would rather use the names of their tribes. (We have used the term "North American Indians" for our series to distinguish this group of people from the inhabitants of India.)

Even the definition of what makes a person "Indian" varies. The U.S. government recognizes certain groups as tribal nations (almost 500 in all). Each nation then decides how it will enroll people as members of that tribe. Tribes may require a particular amount of Indian blood, tribal membership of the father or the mother, or other *criteria*. Some enrolled tribal members who are legally "Indian" may not look Native at all; many have blond hair and blue eyes and others have clearly African features. At the same time, there are thousands of Native people whose tribes have not yet been officially recognized by the government.

We have done our best to write books that are as free from stereotypes as possible. But you as the reader also play a part. After reading one of these books, we hope you won't think: "The Cheyenne are all like this" or "Iroquois are all like that." Each person in this world is unique, whatever their culture. Stereotypes shut people's minds—but these books are intended to open your mind. North American Indians today have much wisdom and beauty to offer.

Some people consider American Indians to be a historical topic only, but Indians today are living, contributing members of North American society. The contributions of the various Indian cultures enrich our world—and North America would be a very different place without the Native people who live there. May they never be lost in North America's "big, wide river"!

At the Cherokee Cultural Center in Talequa, Oklahoma, a recreation of an ancient dwelling shows how the Cherokee people once lived.

Chapter 1

History

In April of 1540, a ragged band of nearly six hundred Spaniards led by Hernando de Soto struggled through what would become the state of Georgia. They were moving quickly, spurred on by tales of gold and silver to the east, when they stumbled across a people they recorded as the "Chalaque." Despite the natives' obvious poverty, they lavished the Spanish with gifts of hundreds of rabbits, partridges, hens, and dogs, which the Spanish gratefully accepted, having already exhausted the small supply of meat they had brought with them from Cuba. In return, De Soto presented the chief with a cannon and a pair of pigs—and then he and his army continued their trek east in search of riches.

This encounter, barely noted by the Spanish, marks the beginning of European awareness of the Cherokee—but it was by no means the beginning of Cherokee history. Though common features of their language and culture suggest a link with the Iroquois and an origin in the Great Lakes region, the Cherokee appear to have begun a gradual southward *migration* a few thousand years ago. At the time of first contact with Europeans, they

An artist's image of a long-ago Cherokee.

occupied a region spanning at least seven modern-day states, an area more than half the size of Texas. For the most part, the tribe prospered in the region, developing a rich culture and society of their own, while continuing to embrace useful *innovations* from neighboring tribes and later from the European colonists.

After the meeting with the Spanish, the Cherokee had little contact with

Europeans for more than a hundred years. In 1673, English from Virginia visited the tribe, and trade between the Cherokee and the English began. While both sides were eager to see this happen, it also spawned numerous conflicts. Some were minor, simple misunderstandings that were easily resolved through negotiations. But as more and more European powers moved into the area, the Cherokee were inevitably drawn into the accompanying political snarls, sometimes with disastrous results.

At the root of many of these problems was the *autonomous* nature of the Cherokee towns. The English, in particular, saw the Cherokee as a single nation, and conflicts occasionally erupted when the colonists assumed that an agreement made with one town applied automatically to another. The Cherokee themselves experienced a similar confusion, seeing all the British colonies as merely "English," rather than as separate states that could *negotiate* agreements independently.

The evolution of a unified Cherokee Nation in fact owes much to this confusing situation. In 1721, the English coaxed the Cherokee into appointing a single man as a sort of "trade commissioner" with whom they could negotiate issues of commerce. Over the years, this position evolved into today's "principal chief," the head of the modern central government.

Although many early encounters were unfriendly, the Cherokee were quick to realize the need to coexist with the Europeans. They were one of a handful of tribes that began to adopt European styles of clothing and modern farm animals and crops, in part as an attempt to ease tensions and fit in with the growing European population. Because of this, the settlers referred to the Cherokee as one of the "Five Civilized Tribes."

Rather than truly being *assimilated* into European culture, the Cherokee incorporated elements of it into their own traditions, creating a way of life that sometimes paralleled European society. Europeans commented on the tribe's commitment to education and willingness to accept or adapt new ideas and ways of doing things, from writing, to clothing, and even religion. Christian missionaries were active and often welcomed among the Cherokee.

For a while, this European strategy of "civilizing" seemed to work. While carving out their own settlements, Europeans were glad to trade with the Cherokee and learn the ways that had allowed the native people to survive on the land for so many years; the white folk felt less threatened by the Cherokee than they did by the more "savage" tribes. But as the settlers became more at home and their populations grew, friction between whites and Cherokees increased. Following the American Revolution, settlers

Light streams through the smoke hole in a recreated ancient Cherokee dwelling.

pushed westward, and competition with the Cherokee for land and game increased considerably. As early as 1795, small groups of Cherokee had succumbed to the mounting pressure and moved west; by the early 1800s, a sizable community had developed in northwestern Arkansas and eastern Oklahoma. Here, in 1824, a silversmith named Sequoyah settled after introducing an innovation that sets the Cherokee apart from other tribes.

When Sequoyah still lived in Georgia, he had become fascinated with the white man's ability to communicate on paper, or "talking leaves," and in 1809 he began to experiment with the idea of a written form for the Cherokee language. While serving in the American army in the War of 1812, he became convinced of the necessity of such a script after seeing how the white soldiers could write letters home to their families and read military orders for themselves. He returned home determined to find a way his people could do the same.

Sequoyah became obsessed with the idea, secluding himself for days at a time to work on the script with his daughter, Ayoka. He endured ridicule and accusations of witchcraft, but in 1821 he unveiled the product of his labor, an eighty-six–character alphabet composed of symbols taken from English, as well as many of his own creation.

Initial reactions were mixed, but after a demonstration to a group of tribal elders, the Cherokee people officially adopted the alphabet. Within a few years, virtually all Cherokee could read and write their own language (a much greater proportion than existed at the time among their white neighbors). Books and newspapers were published, and important religious and legal documents were translated into Cherokee.

Despite these hopeful developments, the Cherokee stood at the brink of one of the most disastrous ages in their history. In the 1830s, gold was discovered in Georgia, and the tragic era of Indian Removals began. Hostilities flared as whites sought to take Native lands. The Cherokees resisted the removals, taking their case all the way to the U.S. Supreme Court, where the controversy was eventually decided in their favor. President Andrew Jackson, however, chose to ignore the Court's decision, saying that Chief Justice "Marshall has made his decision. Let him enforce it."

At this point, some Cherokee, a group later to be known as the Treaty Party, became convinced that removal was inevitable and gave in to the

Cherokee Cultural Center in Talequah, Oklahoma, has preserved the cabin where Sequoyah once lived.

What's Up with the Turbans?

Probably the best-known images of any Cherokee are those of Sequoyah, who is virtually always pictured wearing what appears to be a turban and blue jacket of European design. Both were, in fact, common clothing among Cherokee of that era, though not the tribe's original dress. Although some have claimed the turban as evidence of pre-European contact by Arabs, the real origin of the outfit was more recent.

When the first delegation of Cherokee visited England, the tattooed heads and bodies of the men were deemed too savage and frightening for their audience with the Royal Family. To cover up these markings, they were given English smoking jackets and turbans, such as those worn by the Muslim servants of the royal household. For whatever reason, these styles caught on among the people of the Five Civilized Tribes and continue to be part of cultural dress among the Cherokee.

demands from the government. The treaty, known as the Treaty of New Echota or the Removal Treaty, exchanged all Cherokee lands in the east for five million dollars and seven million acres in what is today northeastern Oklahoma, along with a promise that this land would never be included within the boundaries of any state or territory. This group, while containing some prominent Cherokee, had no real authority and did not represent the tribal government. In spite of this, the U.S. government declared the treaty binding on *all* Cherokee, and the Senate *ratified* the treaty.

The Treaty Party began to move westward to the new lands, but most other Cherokee, under Principal Chief John Ross, refused to leave the state. In response, the state of Georgia passed a series of laws called the "Anti-Cherokee Laws," designed to make life difficult for the remaining Cherokee. These laws forbade Cherokee from mining gold on their own land, prevented them from testifying in court against whites, and prevented non-Cherokees from entering Cherokee Nation territory without first signing a sworn oath of loyalty to the state of Georgia. This last requirement applied even to missionaries and others already living within Cherokee territory. Still, many Cherokee stubbornly refused to leave.

Finally, in 1838, disregarding the ruling of the Supreme Court and the objections of many Americans, President Andrew Jackson ordered thousands of Cherokee men, women, and children rounded up and marched over a thousand miles to Indian Territory, now the state of Oklahoma.

Thousands died in the roundup and subsequent imprisonment in camps, suffering through perhaps the worst drought in the area's recorded history. Conditions in camps were desperate, with poor sanitation and rampant sickness. Realizing that removal was now unavoidable, Ross requested that the Cherokee Nation be allowed to manage the *exodus* itself. The government agreed, and the Cherokee in the camps were divided into thirteen "waves," each led by an appointed "captain." Nearly two thousand Cherokee died during the march west, an average of two people per each mile they traveled; their journey would become known as the "Trail of Tears." Despite Ross's successful plea to the U.S. government for food and clothing, the Cherokee were ill equipped to handle the harsh winter and found themselves trapped by ice floes on the eastern side of the Mississippi River. By the time they reached Oklahoma, many Cherokee had died, and many hundreds more died of sickness and exhaustion shortly after arrival. By some estimates, nearly a quarter of the Cherokee population was dead by the time the last of the tribe had arrived in Oklahoma.

The pillars from the original Cherokee Seminary, the first such school for girls built west of the Mississippi.

The years immediately following removal were marked with violence and disagreements; the wounds caused by the removal linger even today. Angry tribe members murdered several members of the Treaty Party. Although most of the western Cherokee already living in the area welcomed the new arrivals, many of the newcomers were opposed to unifying into a single nation, and sometimes violence broke out. In 1839, despite a series of assassinations by Cherokee opposed to unification, the Cherokee Act of Union officially brought together the eastern and western Cherokee into a united Cherokee Nation, with its capital at Tahlequah.

In spite of the ongoing strife, the new arrivals set about clearing land and establishing villages and farms, abandoning the traditional building styles in favor of the designs prevalent in America at the time. Continuing a long tradition of equal opportunity in education, they built the Cherokee Nation Male and Female Seminaries. The female seminary was in fact the first secondary school for girls west of the Mississippi River. Eventually, most Cherokee began to settle into their new lives.

Unfortunately, they were not to have peace for long. Though there were fewer slaves in the Indian Territory than in most Southern states, the issue of slavery was still a *contentious* one among the Cherokee. This, along with changing social patterns, began to strain the fabric of Cherokee society, which found itself separating into two groups: a wealthier one that favored slavery and large-scale agriculture, often *bilingual* and affiliated with the Southern Baptist Church, and another group that opposed slavery and tended toward more traditional ways of life and affiliation with the Northern Baptists. This second group began to feel increasingly *marginalized*, and their traditional culture was threatened. In response, a secret society appeared in their churches in 1858.

Called the Keetoowah Society, it emphasized the importance of Cherokee traditions and a doctrine of mutual aid. Members would pool their resources to help those members who were sick or destitute, even care for them personally if necessary. Their meetings were full of ceremony and complex rituals. Many have compared them to the activities of the Freemasons of today, of which some of the society's founders were members. While the Keetoowah Society did succeed in bettering the lot of these more traditional people—and it may also be responsible for preserving some of the Cherokee traditions that survive today—it could not prevent the eventual split that fractured the Cherokee Nation.

The Civil War, beginning in 1861, divided the Cherokee just as it did the

a	e	i	o	u	v
D *a*	R *e*	T *i*	Ꭷ *o*	O *u*	i *v*
Ꭶ *ga* Ꭺ *ka*	Ᏸ *ge*	Ᏻ *gi*	A *go*	J *gu*	E *gv*
Ꭲ *ha*	Ꭿ *he*	Ꭹ *hi*	F *ho*	Ꭶ *hu*	Ꮂ *hv*
W *la*	Ꮅ *le*	P *li*	G *lo*	M *lu*	Ꮈ *lv*
Ꮊ *ma*	Ꮉ *me*	H *mi*	Ꮋ *mo*	Ꮏ *mu*	
Ꮎ *na* Ꮏ *hna* G *nah*	Ꮑ *ne*	Ꮒ *ni*	Z *no*	Ꮔ *nu*	O *nv*
Ꮖ *qua*	Ꮗ *que*	Ꮘ *qui*	Ꮙ *quo*	Ꮚ *quu*	Ꮛ *quv*
Ꮜ *sa* Ꭲ *s*	Ꮞ *se*	Ꮟ *si*	Ꮠ *so*	Ꮡ *su*	R *sv*
Ꮣ *da* Ꮤ *ta*	Ꮥ *de* Ꮦ *te*	Ꮧ *di* Ꮨ *ti*	V *do*	S *du*	Ꮫ *dv*
Ꮬ *dla* Ꮭ *tla*	L *tle*	C *tli*	Ꮰ *tlo*	Ꮱ *tlu*	P *tlv*
Ꮳ *tsa*	Ꮴ *tse*	Ir *tsi*	K *tso*	Ꮷ *tsu*	C *tsv*
Ꮹ *wa*	Ꮺ *we*	Ꮻ *wi*	Ꮼ *wo*	Ꮽ *wu*	6 *wv*
Ꮿ *ya*	B *ye*	Ꮑ *yi*	Ꮙ *yo*	G *yu*	B *yv*

Sequoyah's Syllabary

The written language developed by Sequoyah is not truly an alphabet, but rather what is called a "syllabary." Instead of each letter representing a single sound, as in English, Cherokee letters each stand for a syllable. Although such a system requires more letters, it means that pronunciation is very literal, and any Cherokee speaker can learn to read and write with complete accuracy by merely memorizing the symbols.

Modern linguists are impressed by the simple elegance of Sequoyah's system and have successfully applied the same syllabary to a number of other languages without written forms around the world.

We will never let our hold to this land go.

To let it go would be like throwing away the mother that gave us birth.

John Ross
Cherokee

rest of the nation, setting siblings and cousins against one another. Despite pleas for *neutrality* by Chief Ross, a member of the Keetoowah Society, both Union and Confederate Cherokee regiments were formed. Though some were involved in conflicts outside of Oklahoma, these Cherokee units mostly fought each other, often raiding the homes and farms of their own people in search of food and fuel. Following the Union's victory in 1865,

Chiefs for a Day

The chiefs appointed for the Cherokee by the president of the United States served primarily only to add an official air to agreements between the Cherokee people and the government. Most served literally for only one day, and their main qualification was usually simply a willingness to cooperate with the federal government. Seven of these "Chiefs for a Day" served between statehood and the reappointment of former one-day chief Jesse Milam in 1943.

Name	Length of Term	Dates
Andrew Cunningham	Chief for 17 days	November 8–25, 1919
Edward Fry	Chief for 1 day	June 23, 1923
Richard Choate	Chief for 1 day	1925
Charles Hunt	Chief for 1 day	December 27, 1928
Oliver Brewer	Chief for 1 day	May 26, 1931
William Hastings	Chief for 1 day	January 22, 1936
Jesse Milam	Chief for 1 day	April 14, 1942 (first appointment)

the families of many who had fought for the Confederacy fled to Texas and Arkansas, though some would return in later years.

The years following the Civil War were full of changes for the Cherokee. Forced to negotiate peace with the U.S. government, the Cherokee signed a treaty that limited tribal land rights and eliminated the possibility of a Cherokee state. There was talk of resettling *emancipated* slaves in Indian Territory, but Congress eventually relented to the demands of non-Indian settlers who wanted access to the rich lands. In 1887, an act was passed requiring individual ownership of lands that had once been held in common by entire tribes in the Indian Territory, allotting tracts to individual tribe members; this caused a major disruption of traditional society. It also paved the way for the opening of unassigned lands to white settlers, who streamed into Indian Territory as the nation expanded westward, their numbers supplemented by immigrants from Ireland, Germany, and eastern Europe. Some freed slaves, many of them the former slaves of tribe members, also settled in the area, either taking part in the government land runs for non-Indians or accepting allotments as tribe members.

The next few years saw a slow breakdown of the traditional Cherokee nation, as more whites moved into Indian Territory and the U.S. government stripped tribal governments of more and more powers. In 1898, the Curtis Act abolished tribal courts, and in 1907, Indian Territory became part of the new state of Oklahoma. For most practical purposes, statehood put an end to actual tribal governments. The last elected chief, William C. Rogers, died in 1917, and for the next fifty-five years the only chiefs were those occasionally appointed by the president of the United States to sign official documents.

Statehood was a traumatic experience for many of the tribes living there. The Cherokee were no exception. One day they were citizens of an independent Cherokee state, the next, residents of the United States. Indians who had lived for generations under their own laws were suddenly subjected to the *intricacies* of American law, and many were overwhelmed or taken advantage of by unscrupulous whites. Indians were swindled and tricked into signing confusing contracts, and many lost their property or savings to legal technicalities.

Before statehood, the Cherokee Nation had produced more college graduates than the states of Arkansas and Texas combined. By 1970, the average Cherokee adult had only five years of schooling. Poverty, once unknown among the Cherokee, was now rampant. Suddenly lost in a society unlike their own, many Cherokee began to worry about their people's survival.

While many Cherokee became prominent politicians in the young state's government, officially there no longer was a Cherokee nation, except for the occasional appointed chief. Despite the lack of a recognized tribal government, several groups began to work to organize an unofficial system of government for the tribe. In an election not recognized by the U.S. government, Jesse Milam was elected principal chief in 1938. While the election was not official, President Franklin Roosevelt eventually did appoint him principal chief in 1941, ending the series of "Chiefs for a Day." Many consider this the turning point in the tribe's history, marking the beginning of the long task of healing the damages of the past several hundred years.

Even though his government had been sanctioned by the U.S. government, or perhaps even because it had been, many Cherokee still did not see Jesse Milam as the legitimate political leader of the Cherokee people. As a result, a group of more traditional Cherokee sought recognition under

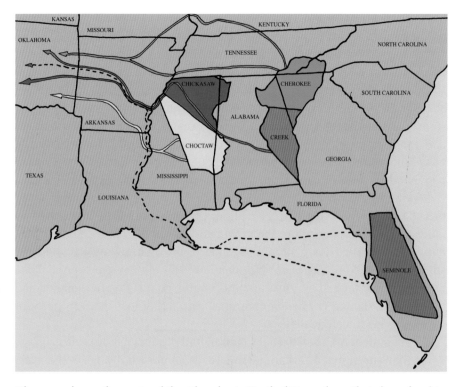

The map shows the route of the Cherokee's Trail of Tears from their homeland to Oklahoma. Note that the Cherokee were not the only ones to be removed from their land; other tribes had their own "Trail of Tears."

the Oklahoma Indian General Welfare Act of 1936, which allowed approved groups all the rights and privileges of federally recognized tribes. Finally, this group, under the name United Keetoowah Band of Cherokee Indians in Oklahoma (UKB), was granted approval in 1950.

While many credit the UKB with doing much to protect the rights of the Cherokee and easing the transition to statehood, in many ways this new tribal government only confused things further. Unclear laws and ignorance on the part of both the Cherokee and the federal government often kept the UKB from being effective, and in many cases, the federal government was unsure whether to deal with the Cherokee Nation government, the UKB government, or both. The Oklahoma State government tended to ignore federal Indian law entirely. Many Cherokee communities began to avoid any entanglement with state and federal law as completely as possible, returning to the ancient Cherokee tradition of independent communities living in isolation from the rest of the world as much as possible.

But the Cherokee held on. During the Nixon administration, the U.S. government finally recognized the Cherokee Nation's elections, and the tribal government slowly became more effective. A new tribal office complex was built, and plans were laid for a Cherokee heritage center in Tahlequah. Completed in 1963, the center houses a museum and *archive*, as well as an outdoor amphitheater and replica villages.

Today, the Cherokee Nation of Oklahoma has more than 220,000 members. It has its own elected government and its own judicial system. The government now has the authority to administer federal money by itself, rather than having to trust the judgment of the federal government. Other federally recognized Cherokee nations are much smaller. The UKB continues to coexist with the Cherokee Nation in eastern Oklahoma, while the Eastern Band of Cherokee Indians lives on part of the tribe's traditional homeland in western North Carolina. Smaller Cherokee communities, not officially recognized by the national government, are scattered across the country and even into Mexico, and there are Cherokee living in most major cities in the United States. Some of these are officially acknowledged by the states they are found in, though many are not. Members of all of these Cherokee groups are active in government, the military, business, and entertainment, and have made major contributions to the United States and the world.

The years since the Europeans' appearance in North America have not been easy ones for the Cherokee. Still, they have survived, and many consider the tribe to have been making a steady comeback since Oklahoma's statehood. Only time will tell what the future holds.

The bear plays a central role in many Cherokee stories.

Chapter 2

Stories of the People

For many Cherokee, the events described in the previous chapter are only part of their history. Long before contact with Europeans, the Cherokee told stories of their past—some historical, some to help explain the workings of the natural world around them, and some, most likely, merely to entertain. Because the early Cherokee had no written language, these stories were passed down orally, told and retold over the centuries, changing slowly through the generations but still preserving the traditions and knowledge of the ancient times. This tradition continues with modern Cherokee storytellers, like Choogie Kingfisher, who not only collects and preserves the ancient stories but also travels to schools and communities to retell the stories.

Stories did not just preserve important knowledge about the past and the origins of the world, they also worked to teach each person his or her place in the world, as a person, as a Cherokee, and as a member of a particular clan. Details of all of these stories can vary greatly from family to family and place to place. There are no right or wrong versions.

The tale that follows is the Cherokee story of the beginning of the world.

In the beginning, the universe was divided into two worlds. One was a heavenly realm, called *Ga-lun-la-ti*, while the other was a dark, lower world inhabited by forces of evil and darkness. Ga-lun-la-ti was filled with many different living things, human, animal, and plant, all of which lived together quite happily, speaking to each other in the Cherokee tongue. The Earth at that time was just a ball of water populated by giant fish and reptiles. Everything was in a state of equilibrium, the things of light balanced by the things of shadow.

In the center of Ga-lun-la-ti grew a huge tree, which lit up the world and the dark waters below it. It was here that the Creator lived, tending the plants and animals. He lived alone, and when his work among the plants and animals was done, he would rest by the tree, admiring the world, both above and below. But he eventually became lonely, and he longed for someone to sit with him in the evenings and delight in his creation along with him.

So one day the Creator made for himself a daughter, a young woman of incredible beauty. He worried that she would be bored and lonely without a companion to play with while he worked, so he made a man in his own likeness as well and taught the two of them all the things he knew. They were called First Woman and First Man.

Although the Creator loved his daughter, he found that she was a constant distraction. She was always laughing and asking questions, and despite her father's warning, her curiosity often got the better of her; she would even climb and play on the great tree. First Man told her not to do so, but every day she would climb far up into the tree. One day, she found a hole at the bottom of the trunk. First Man tried to stop her, but she pushed him aside, and crawled into the hole.

Soon the Creator finished his work for the day; when he returned home, he noticed First Woman was missing. First Man told him, "I told her not to go into the hole at the base of the tree, but she would not listen." The Creator rushed to the edge and saw his daughter plummeting down toward the ball of water below, for the hole had led straight out the bottom of Ga-lun-la-ti!

The Creator called for the birds, and they created a huge blanket with their wings in which they caught her, saving her from drowning. But the birds did not know where to put her. Finally, the grandfather of all turtles who lived in the waters, surfaced. "Place her on my back," he said, and the birds gently set the young woman, who was now known as "Sky Woman,"

First Man and First Woman

First Man and First Women exemplify the traditional roles of Cherokee men and women as hunters and farmers. First Man was also known as the Great Hunter, while First Woman was sometimes known as the Corn Mother, and one of her names, *Selu*, is the same as the Cherokee word for corn. In one tale, she is even able to produce corn and beans from her body. Cherokee women were skilled agriculturists, tending gardens of corn, beans, and squash. The men's only role was to help occasionally with heavy labor, such as removing rocks. When harvest came, it belonged only to the woman and her children; whether or not she shared it with her husband was entirely up to her. He, however, was expected to provide her with meat, regardless.

on his shell. The young woman was glad to be safe, but she thought the turtle's back was too small and awfully bare. The muskrat offered his help, and dove down to the bottom of the waters. He scooped up huge handfuls of mud and spread it on the turtle's back. When Sky Woman touched it, it grew out in all directions, becoming the lands of the Earth as we know it today. The Creator sent other animals and plants to help her and her descendants.

When the Sky Woman was pleased with this new world, the Creator sent First Man down to be her husband and help her care for the new land. At first they were happy, but eventually they began to argue.

After one particularly bitter argument, Sky Woman grabbed her belongings and walked away from her husband. "I am going to find somewhere else to live," she said. "You are lazy and you ignore me all the time." She turned her back on him and left.

Soon, First Man began to regret his harsh words, and he tried to catch up with his wife so he could apologize. But after struggling to reach her, he realized that she was simply too far ahead of him. He cried to the Creator, "Slow her down, Creator! I want to tell her how much she means to me!"

Long-ago Cherokee lived in dwellings like this.

The Creator heard his cries and answered, "Is her soul one with yours?"

"We have been one since time began," First Man answered. "We have been one since you breathed life into us, and we will remain one until the end of time."

The Creator was touched by the man's words, and he intervened to stop her. As the woman walked, he caused plants to grow at her feet to slow her down. On one side of her, blackberries sprang up, and on the other, huckleberries, but she avoided them and walked on. He made gooseberries and serviceberries grow on either side of her, but she kept going. Finally the Creator grabbed a handful of strawberry plants that were growing in his garden and cast them down in front of her, where they began to bloom and ripen. The berries looked so good, Sky Woman paused to try one. As she picked and ate the berries, her anger disappeared, and while she filled her basket with the fruit, she began to wish that her husband was there to share it with her. Just then, First Man appeared, his heart full of gladness to have found his wife. With a smile, she took a strawberry from her basket and placed it in his mouth. He smiled with pleasure and gave thanks to the Creator. Together they returned home hand in hand, eating strawberries along the way.

As mentioned in the previous chapter, at the time of first contact with Europeans, each Cherokee town was a self-governing unit. However, according to one tale, this was not always the case. Many years ago, it is said, the whole Cherokee tribe was ruled by a powerful group of priests called the *Ani-Kutani*. Although they may have originally been a religious society, they eventually became a hereditary group, considered to be a separate clan. The Creator had initially granted them great powers to do good things, but they eventually became corrupt and cruel.

One day, a hunter returned from a long hunting trip and was upset when he could not find his wife. He asked the other townspeople where she had gone, and they told him that while he was away, the priests had come and taken her. Enraged, the hunter gathered up the other young men of the village to discuss what should be done about the Ani-Kutani. Everyone agreed that priests had taken advantage of them for too long and that finally they had gone too far. The young men gathered up their weapons and killed all the priests. The responsibility for religion was given to the *medicine men*, who could not pass their position on to their sons, and political power was vested in the appointed chiefs of each village. Thus, each town came to have its own government, which was elected rather than hereditary.

One of the most important Cherokee stories is that of Keetoowah, the original town in modern-day North Carolina from which some say all Cherokee originated (others say there were seven "mother towns," of which Keetoowah was merely the most important). In fact, one of the early names the Cherokee used for themselves was *Ani-Kituwagi*, which meant "Keetoowah People." When the town's population grew, groups of people moved out of Keetoowah to build new towns. Many believe this is why each Cherokee town came to have the same seven clans. The meaning of the word "Keetoowah" was long kept from outsiders, and some say it was forgotten entirely, although others have suggested that it means "protected" or "covered."

Clingman's Dome and the Era of Removals

Perched along the border between North Carolina and Tennessee, Clingman's Dome features in more recent Cherokee history as well as in ancient stories, including an episode that is very important to the Eastern Cherokee today. In 1838, an old Cherokee farmer named Tsali and his sons shot a white soldier while resisting the family's expulsion from their farm. They fled into the hills, hiding in a cave at the base of Clingman's Dome. Many other Cherokee fled as well, hiding through the hills of their native lands.

General Winfield Scott, who was overseeing the Cherokee removal, realized that the Cherokee had the advantage in the hills, which they knew far better than the soldiers. Scott decided it was not worth the lives it would cost to hunt down all the Cherokee, but he refused to let Tsali and his sons get away with killing one of his men. So he sent William Thomas, a trader who had grown up among the Cherokee, to talk with Tsali, who knew and trusted him. Tsali and his sons agreed to turn themselves over in exchange for the right of the other Cherokee to go on living in the mountains. Tsali, his brother-in-law, and his two sons were executed, but General Scott allowed the rest of the Cherokee to remain free. It is those fugitives who are the ancestors of today's Eastern Band.

Whatever the meaning, the word today suggests everything traditional and sacred to the Cherokee; it carries the sense of looking back to the earliest days, before the changes brought about by European contact. Keetoowah was, after all, the source of everything Cherokee.

Tradition holds that while migrating southward, the elders of the tribe stopped at *Kuwo-yi*, meaning Mulberry Place, atop what is now known as Clingman's Dome. They reached a spot where the trees were scorched by lightning strikes, a sign of heavenly powers, and they waited for many days to hear the voices of the Thunders. Finally, the Thunders spoke to them, giving the medicine men the moral codes and clan law that are the foundations of Cherokee tradition. Some even say that the Thunders foretold the coming of the Europeans and the Trail of Tears. Whatever the exact message, it is for this reason that Clingman's Dome is referred to by some as the "Cherokee *Mount Sinai*."

After receiving the message from the Thunders, the elders rejoined the rest of the tribe and traveled about thirty miles to a suitable site for a new town. There they built Keetoowah. It was here that the new law was put into effect, marking the beginning of the Cherokee as a separate, defined people.

Kuwo-yi is significant to the Cherokee for another reason as well. There, some say, the bears met in council. The Cherokee were impressed with the cleverness of bears, and considered them to be quite human, ascribing to them in stories many human abilities and thoughts. According to one tale, the bears themselves were originally Cherokee.

Legend has it that long ago there was a clan called the *Ani-Tsa-gu-hi*. One member of the clan, a young boy, would often leave the village, spending all day long in the woods and mountains, eventually staying so

Cherokee Robert Lewis recreates the arrowheads and stone tools used by his ancestors.

long that he would no longer even eat at home. His parents were worried, and they became even more worried when they noticed he was beginning to grow black hair all over his body. "Why do you want to spend all day in the woods?" they asked. "Why don't you stay at home?"

But the boy would not listen. "I find plenty to eat out there, and it's better than the corn and beans we have here," he said. "Pretty soon I'm going to go into the woods and stay there." His parents begged him not to leave, but he refused, pointing out that he now looked so different he could not stay if he wanted to. "There is plenty for everyone out there if you want to come with me," he said. "If you do, you must first fast for seven days."

His parents went to the elders of the clan, and a council was convened. After much discussion, it was decided. "Here we must always work hard, and even then there seems like there is never enough," they said. "There, he says there is plenty, and it is easy to have without any work. We will go with him." So they all left the settlement and went out into the woods to begin fasting.

When the other clans heard what they were doing, they sent messengers to them, asking them to come back. The messengers found that the Ani-Tsa-gu-hi were already changing, having had no human food for seven days, and they were by then covered in hair. When the messengers pled with them, the Ani-Tsa-gu-hi said only, "We are going where there is plenty to eat. From now on, we will be called *Yonva*, and when you are hungry, come and call for us, and we will come and give our flesh over to you. Do not be worried about killing us because we will live always." Then they taught the messengers special songs with which to call the bears, songs that bear hunters sing even to this day. When they finished learning the songs, the messengers turned to return to their villages, and the Ani-Tsa-gu-hi continued into the woods. When the messengers looked back at where they had been, all they saw was a group of black bears walking into the woods.

Other Cherokee stories tell of people turning into bears. In one, a hunter is lost and lives among the bears for a year. When he returns to his town, he is half bear and must fast to become a man again. The bears feature prominently in many other stories, as well. One such tale recounts the beginning of disease—and medicine.

Originally people lived in harmony with all the animals, speaking with them in Cherokee. However, as time went by, the people grew in number and spread out over the world, and the animals began to feel cramped for space. Things became even worse when the humans learned to make weapons and began to hunt the larger animals for their hides. The smaller animals, while not hunted, were often crushed accidentally or out of spite. Finally, the animals decide to meet in council to decide how to keep themselves safe.

The first to meet were the bears, who met at *Kuow-yi*. The White Bear, the old Chief, led the council. One by one, the bears described all the horrible things people had done to them and their friends. There were stories of bears being killed, skinned, and eaten. At last it was decided: there would be war against the humans. One bear asked what kind of weapons the humans were using against them. "Bows and arrows," cried the rest of the bears at once. "What are they made of?" came the next question. "The bow is made of wood, but the string is made of our entrails," replied one of the bears.

The bears decided they would make a bow of their own and see if they could learn to use the same weapon as the people did. One of the bears agreed to sacrifice himself, and his entrails were used as a string. The other bears found a piece of locust wood and made a bow.

One bear drew the bow and let fly an arrow, but his long claws caught on the string and the shot was ruined. He was very frustrated, but another bear suggested clipping his claws, after which the arrows flew straight and true. All the bears were ready to trim their claws, but Chief White Bear stopped them. He pointed out that they needed their claws to climb trees. "One of us has already given his life," he said, "and if we cut off our claws, we will all starve together. We should simply use the teeth and claws we were given by the Creator, for it is obvious that the people's weapons were not made for us."

The deer held their council next. They decided that every time a hunter killed a deer, they would curse him with painful rheumatism, unless he asked the deer for forgiveness. They sent word to the Cherokee to inform them of this rule. From then on, whenever a hunter shoots a deer, their chief, Little Deer, rushes to the spot and asks the spirit of the deer if it has heard the hunter's prayers for pardon. If yes, then the hunter is allowed to go unharmed. If no, Little Deer secretly follows the hunter home and strikes him with arthritis. So all Cherokee hunters are sure to remember to ask for pardon when they kill a deer.

The fish and reptiles held their council next. They decided to plague their victims with bad dreams. The snakes sent dreams of crawling snakes, breathing their foul breath. The fish sent dreams of decaying fish to make people lose their appetites and die of hunger.

The last to meet were the small animals. The birds, insects, and small mammals gathered together, led by their chief, the grub worm. Each told his tale of abuse by the humans. Only the ground squirrel, who kept out of the way of the humans and was too small to be worth hunting, said anything in the people's defense. The others were so angry they tore at him with their claws, leaving the stripes that are visible on his back to this day. Then the animals began to name disease after disease.

Only the plants remained friendly to human beings. When the growing things heard about all of the animals' plans, they agreed that they would help the people. Each plant decided to help provide a cure for some disease, saying, "I will appear and help the people when they call upon me." This is the origin of medicine. Every plant has a use, though many are no longer known. Sometimes when a doctor does not know which medicine to use, the spirit of the plant will tell the person who is sick.

Today, the Cherokee are still great believers in the interrelatedness of all things. Their traditions stress the need to treat all of creation with respect. Many of their oral traditions revolve around this theme.

The Cherokee's sense of history is wide and rich, extending beyond their current geographic location. Some of their oral traditions, like the story that follows, explain the stars' beginnings. These stories give the Cherokee an ongoing sense of connection to the entire universe.

Long ago, seven boys spent all their time playing *gatayû'stï*, a game that is now called "chunkey." Their mothers told them to stop, but they ignored them. Finally, their mothers collected the stones used in the game and boiled them in the pot with their dinner.

When the boys came home for dinner, their mothers spooned out the boiled stones for them, saying, "Since you prefer to play gatayû'stï instead of working, take these for your dinner."

The boys were upset and went down to the town house. "If our mothers are going to treat us like this, let's go somewhere where they we won't bother them anymore." They began to dance and pray for the spirits to help them. When their mothers looked out to see what was going on, they saw the boys begin to lift off the ground. The mothers ran to pull them down, but all but one was out of reach. One boy's mother caught him with the gatayû'stï pole, but he fell so hard that he sank into the earth and disappeared.

The other six boys circled up into the sky until they were just points of light, where they remain even today as the Pleiades, which the Cherokee call *Ani'tsutsä*, meaning "the Boys." The mother of the boy who had fallen came every morning and evening to mourn at the spot where he had disappeared, leaving the ground wet with her tears. One day, a small green shoot appeared and began to grow until it became a tall tree we call the pine.

While most legends are ancient in origin, told and retold by countless generations of Cherokee, some are more recent. A more recent story tells about a miraculous happening along the Trail of Tears.

Many people died on the journey, and the women wept. The elders knew that the children would not survive if the women could not stay strong, and they prayed to God to help their people and give these mothers strength. In response to their prayers, God caused a plant to spring up wherever a mother's tears had fallen. He told the elders how the plant would grow, expanding rapidly before falling back to the ground so another stem could grow.

The flower was a white rose with a yellow center, representing the white man and the gold he lusted after. The leaves were made of seven leaflets, one for each clan. Its thorns would protect it from those who would remove it, guaranteeing that it would remain as a reminder of the Cherokee in their old homeland.

The next morning, the women looked back down the trail they had traveled and saw the white blossoms dotting their path. When they heard from the elders what God had said, they felt their strength return and knew they would survive to help the children grow and the Cherokee people live on.

These stories and others like them persist in the collective memory of twenty-first-century Cherokee. Whether the stories serve to explain, comfort, or amuse, they are a valuable heritage for they offer a connection to the past even as they give meaning to modern life. These oral traditions help shape the identity of today's Cherokee people.

Wilma Mankiller, a former principal chief of the Cherokee Nation.

Chapter 3

Current Government

Wilma Mankiller, a former principal chief of the Cherokee Nation, once described her job as being like "running a small country, a medium-size corporation, and being a social worker." The tribal governments of the Cherokee essentially do all these things. They pass laws, levy taxes, and hold elections just like most countries. They own and operate businesses. And they provide for the economic and emotional needs of their people.

Today, there are three groups of Cherokee whose governments are recognized by the federal government. The largest by far is the Cherokee Nation of eastern Oklahoma, with more than 220,000 members. The descendants of the few Cherokee that remained in the east form the Eastern Band of Cherokee Indians in North Carolina, with about 12,000 members, and a third group, the United Keetoowah Band, has about 7,700 members.

Legally, only the Eastern Band has a *reservation*. The Cherokee Nation possesses sovereign control of 66,000 acres (approximately 26,720 hectares) of land in eastern Oklahoma, but technically this is a "jurisdictional area." The United Keetoowah Band is unusual in that it is the only

The Cherokee Nation has its own license plates with its tribal seal.

federally acknowledged landless tribe. Most of its members live in eastern Oklahoma, alongside the Cherokee Nation, but the federal government has ruled that they have no jurisdiction in Oklahoma. So they have established a base in Waldron, Arkansas, although the seat of the government remains in Oklahoma.

The Cherokee Nation's capitol is located at Tahlequah, Oklahoma. The government is outlined in its **constitution**, which was adopted June 26, 1976. It outlines a system loosely modeled on that of the United States, with three branches: the executive, legislative, and judicial.

The head of the executive branch is the principal chief. His or her role includes the execution and enforcement of tribal law and overall authority over the day-to-day operations of the Cherokee Nation and all its programs and enterprises. A deputy principal chief, who assumes the role of principal chief in the event of death or resignation, assists him. Both are elected to four-year terms by a majority of voters.

The legislative branch is composed of the Tribal Council. The fifteen members represent the nine districts of the Cherokee Nation. The deputy principal chief heads the Tribal Council, and its primary function is to introduce legislation. Voters in their districts elect the members to four-year terms.

The judicial branch is composed of two courts: the Judicial Appeals Tribunal and the Cherokee District Court. The Cherokee District Court handles legal cases that fall under the jurisdiction of the Cherokee Nation judicial code. The role of the Judicial Appeals Tribunal is similar to that of the U.S. Supreme Court. The principal chief appoints its members, and their job is to resolve disagreements in the interpretation and application of the tribe's constitution.

The Eastern Band has a similar government, comprised of an executive branch, a judicial branch, and a legislative branch. The executive branch is

The official flag of the Cherokee Nation stands in the court house.

The Cherokee Nation has its own judicial branch.

composed of a principal chief and a vice chief, who serve very much the same roles as they do in the Cherokee Nation government. The tribal council is made up of twelve representatives, each representing a different township. Rather than each having a single vote, there are a total of a hundred votes, and each township receives a certain proportion of them based on population. The judicial branch is composed of the Cherokee Supreme Court and the Cherokee Court, which function similarly to the two courts in the Cherokee Nation.

The politics of the Cherokee Nation government have always been turbulent, and recent years have been no exception. When Mankiller ran as deputy principal chief in 1983, with Principal Chief Ross Swimmer, many were so upset at the idea of a female leader that she received numerous death threats during the election campaign. When Swimmer resigned his position in 1985, Mankiller assumed the role of principal chief. Her successor, Joe Byrd, became principal chief through a strange set of circumstances.

When Wilma Mankiller did not run again in 1995, a number of people ran for her position as principal chief. None of these candidates received the necessary 51 percent of the votes required to win, and so a runoff was planned between George Bearpaw and Joe Byrd, the top two candidates in the initial election. Before the runoff election could go forward, however, it was discovered that Bearpaw was ineligible to run because of an earlier felony assault conviction. In a decision akin to that of the Supreme Court decision in a 2000 federal election, the Cherokee Nation Judicial Appeals Tribunal declared that the runoff would go on, but that only votes for Joe Byrd would count, essentially handing him the election by default.

During the following years, Byrd was accused of everything from ignoring the Cherokee Constitution and the Cherokee judicial system to financial impropriety. He fired the Cherokee marshal service and hired his own security guards, touching off an armed standoff and brawl in Tahlequah. Under his leadership, the Cherokee Nation went from a financial surplus to deep deficit. The four years of his term were filled with turmoil and resulted in armed conflict between citizens, former Cherokee Marshals, various law enforcement agencies, and the Bureau of Indian Affairs.

The situation persisted until the heavily monitored election of 1999, in which Chadwick Smith became chief. His administration has worked hard to correct the problems of its predecessors, and many Cherokee believe it has done much to improve the state of the Cherokee Nation.

Becoming a Registered Cherokee

Different tribal governments have different requirements for membership. The Eastern Band maintains a strict requirement that members prove they are at least one-quarter Cherokee. The Cherokee Nation, in Oklahoma, imposes no such restriction on the degree of Cherokee ancestry, and some members are less than one-thousandth Cherokee. However, to be eligible for membership, one must be able to prove descent from an original enrollee listed on the tribal rolls completed by the Dawes Commission between 1899 and 1906. This excludes many people of genuine Cherokee blood whose ancestors were living in nearby areas of Arkansas, Kansas, and Texas. This is a source of great frustration to some and is part of the reason behind the many unrecognized tribes now seeking federal acknowledgment. Some of the unrecognized tribes have less strict requirements for membership, and some have been accused of being of questionable historical authenticity.

The Cherokee Nation's tribal seal.

Like most sovereign nations, the Cherokee Nation requires money to fund its programs and activities. One way it does this is through taxes. Starting in 1990, there has been a Cherokee Nation Tax Commission, which collects taxes on a variety of activities. Sales of cigarettes are taxed, and money is collected from vehicle registrations. In addition, a substantial sum is taken in through issuing Cherokee Nation license plates, which are available to registered members of the tribe living within the boundaries of the Cherokee Nation.

In addition to levying taxes, the Cherokee Nation government owns and operates a number of businesses, which provide a source of revenue for the tribe. Cherokee Nation Industries is a tribally owned corporation with more than 350 employees. It has a number of divisions, including medical services, telecommunication, and cable and wire harness manufacturing, and has contracts with the military, NASA, and Boeing. The company provides both a source of income for the tribe and opportunities for employment for tribal members.

The Cherokee Nation, like many other tribes, also operates casinos, which also provide revenue. There are three casinos in eastern Oklahoma, and a third in North Carolina, operated by the Eastern Band. While some Cherokee, particularly those in religious and traditional groups, oppose gambling for moral reasons, the casinos are popular with many tourists and provide a significant stream of revenue for the tribe.

With the money collected from these sources, the Cherokee Nation provides its members with a wide range of services. Programs range from assistance for home construction to health services and educational initiatives.

Education has been an important priority throughout Cherokee history. The tribe operates Sequoyah High School, an Indian boarding school, and also provides a variety of other programs in language and cultural education for children and adults. It also administers federal educational aid for public schools. Some have criticized this arrangement, suggesting that the tribal government has no business being in public education. Critics worry that funds are being handled poorly and that those in charge of education for the tribe have little experience with public schools.

Citizens of the various Cherokee nations are, of course, also citizens of the United States, and so the federal government also plays an important role in the lives of the people. The Bureau of Indian Affairs (BIA) manages relations between the national government and the tribes, and handles the various federal programs that fund some tribal programs. An important example of such a program is the Johnson–O'Malley Act, which provides educational funds for things like school supplies, language instruction, resources for home schooling, tutoring, and career services.

While many Cherokee have been involved in the state and federal governments, Native American turnout in elections has historically been poor. The reasons for this are not entirely clear, but many point to the tradition of decentralized authority among the ancient Cherokee and continuing distrust of the federal government. Many older members of the tribe vote Republican largely because Andrew Jackson was a Democrat—despite the fact that the Democratic Party has changed drastically since Jackson's day. Still, efforts have been made to improve voter participation, and many credit improved Native American turnout in Oklahoma as being critical to the outcome of some recent congressional races there.

The Cherokee's tribal governments are no longer the *wards* of the federal government they once were. Today, the tribal governments have restored to the Cherokee a degree of the *sovereignty* they once possessed, alongside but independent of the federal government. These governments form a framework for addressing the specific needs of the Cherokee people and a starting point for correcting the effects of the many wrongs the tribe has suffered.

A church at the Cherokee Cultural Center in Talequah, Oklahoma, reflects the combination of Christianity and Cherokee tradition.

Chapter 4

Religion

Today, most Cherokee think of themselves as Christians, generally members of one of several mainstream Protestant denominations. Some worship in small churches with primarily Cherokee membership, some of which even hold services in the Cherokee language, and many popular hymns have been translated into Cherokee.

The shift from the ancient religious traditions to Christianity began early in the tribe's contacts with Europeans, through the work of missionaries and an active desire by the Cherokees to fit in with the new settlers. The religious change was eased by the fact that many Cherokee considered the new faith to be completely compatible with the old Keetoowah faith, and many practiced both simultaneously or adopted elements from each. "For us," commented one tribal elder, "it was just a new face for the same God."

This parallel observance of both faiths continues today. One Saturday night each month, many Cherokee still attend stomp dances held at one of seven "stomp grounds"—and then get up the next morning and head for church. Some refer to the stomp ground as "the Outdoor Church," and the Christian church as "the Indoor Church." Like most churches, these are both social and religious events.

Although the stomp dance ceremony has quiet and serious moments, much of the time is spent socializing, eating, and getting caught up on the events of the past month. Many families live a long distance from the stomp ground and see each other only once a month. The stomp dance gives them a chance to feel close to other Cherokees, serving to connect them both to the spiritual world and to each other.

Seven stomp grounds are still in use in Oklahoma, though tradition holds that there were once at least twenty-two, each descendants of village council fires in the ancient Cherokee homeland. The Eastern Band of North Carolina has several stomp grounds as well. As the Christian church began to assume much of the role of the council house, the council fires and the stomp dances moved outside town, where they continued secretly. Those **traditionalists** who attended these late night, backcountry ceremonies were known as "Nighthawk Keetoowah."

Each stomp ground has a Chief, who is in charge of the overall operation of the stomp ground and the stomp dance ceremony, and a Second Chief, who acts as his assistant. Despite their titles, they are spiritual authorities, not political ones, and their influence does not extend beyond the stomp ground and their congregations.

The Chief is usually an older man with years of knowledge and training in traditional medicine and Cherokee traditions and stories. He often wears a tall feather sticking up from his hat. The Second Chief is in some ways his **apprentice**, learning the skills he needs to be Chief himself one day as he helps to run the stomp dance. Another person is also appointed to oversee the preparation of the food; the Firekeeper, often quite young, cooks and maintains the fires during the ceremony.

Preparations for the stomp dance begin at dawn with the kindling of the sacred fire. The men sit around and discuss social and political topics, while the women begin working on the meal. Sermons in English and Cherokee are held throughout the day, often focusing on themes of peace and love. Children (and adults) play stickball nearby while the food is prepared.

Stickball is a traditional game similar to lacrosse, but played with two small sticks. While not noticeably filled with religious ritual, the Cherokee consider the stickball game to have religious importance, and no stomp dance can begin without it. In the past, every stickball game began with a

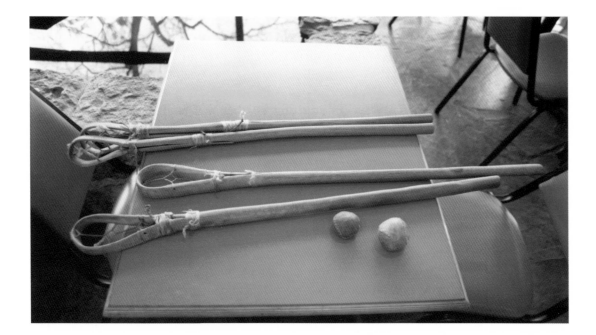

Stickball

Stickball is game played by many of the Southeast Woodlands tribes, including the Cherokee. Games today can be very rough, with everything from hair pulling to headlocks perfectly legal, but in the past they could be positively brutal, with serious injuries frequent and even occasional deaths.

The game is played with a ball similar to a hackey-sack, made of deer hide and stuffed with deer hair. Each player holds a small stick in each hand, curved around into a webbed loop on one end. Participants carry and pass the ball around the field using the sticks, attempting to hit a ball or a metal fish at the top of a tall pole. Teams range from twenty to sixty players each, and the fields used can be immense.

Historically, an unfortunate player who dropped his stick was forced to carry the ball in his teeth, which usually resulted in him being struck in the head in attempts to knock it loose. In today's gentler game, women are sometimes allowed to play using their hands, although men still must use sticks.

Originally, only the tribe's fittest men played the game, which was considered to be training for war. Indeed, its Cherokee name, *A-ne-jo-di*, means "the Little Brother to War." The game was even used as a substitute for armed conflict, settling disputes between tribes and villages, sometimes deciding control of large tracts of land.

ritual dance, and the quality of a team's **conjurer** was considered as important a factor as the ability of the players.

As darkness falls, the stickball games draw to a close, and people gather at the small cook shack where the meal has been laid out, buffet style. The chief of the stomp ground quiets the conversation, and heads are bowed as he delivers a prayer, first in English, then in Cherokee. The English prayer sounds remarkably like a standard Christian prayer, giving thanks to God for food, family, and health, with only the occasional brief reference to some element of Cherokee tradition. Then the meal is served, with guests going first. The foods and drinks are a mix of traditional foods, such as beans and corn bread, and those adopted from Europeans or other tribes in more recent times, such as **fry bread**, chicken, and coffee.

Slowly, people begin to migrate to the arbors. Seven arbors, wooden frames covering several benches and roofed with tree branches, ring a large fire. At one time, each arbor would have housed a specific clan, but today few Cherokees even know their clan affiliation, so people can sit wherever they like. In colder weather, few if any people sit under the arbors at all, preferring to sit on folding chairs clustered around smaller fires behind the arbors.

Turtle shell rattles were once used in the stomp dance. Today they have sometimes been replaced by rattles made from cans.

A Christian church might be called the "Indoor Church" by some Cherokee, while the stomp grounds are the "Outdoor Church."

Before the actual dance begins, all the participants line up to "take medicine." The Chief and Second Chief offer ladles of the medicine, an ancient mixture of water and a number of different plants, a little like a weak tea, which is used for ritual cleansing. The Chief or Second Chief pours the liquid into people's cupped hands seven times, each time pausing for them to rub the liquid over their bodies. Then, the Chief offers the remaining liquid in the ladle, which is swallowed.

After undergoing this cleansing, people return to their seats around the ring of arbors. By this time it is late, nearly eleven o'clock. The central fire blazes brightly as the Chief enters the ring, circling the fire in a counter-clockwise direction. This is important, because tradition dictates that one should never turn one's right shoulder toward the fire. The fire is considered to be a symbol of *Unetlanv*, the Cherokee name for the Creator, and its smoke carries prayers to heaven. In some grounds, it is said that the fire is kindled upon the ashes of ceremonial fires brought over the Trail of Tears. The Cherokees therefore keep their left side, where the heart is located, toward the fire.

Arbors circle the sacred fire at a Cherokee stomp ground.

The Chief meets with the elders, says a few words in Cherokee, and a group of people step into the ring to begin the first dance. The first dance is by invitation only and consists of the Chief, medicine men, and respected elders and members of the congregation. After this, all dances are open to all who would like to participate. It is a relatively simple dance. The participants move in a line that winds around the fire, stepping with a sort of stomping, shuffling motion. Participants mimic the motions of the leader at the front of the line, often raising their hands or bowing toward the fire as they dance.

The women, who usually make up every other person in the line if numbers allow, wear rattles on their ankles that set the beat as they dance. These rattles are traditionally made of turtle shells filled with river pebbles. While many still use this style, some people, particularly young women and girls, use metal cans instead of shells.

The songs sung during the stomp dance are ancient. The meanings of many have been lost because they are written in a language older than the modern Cherokee tongue, but the words have been faithfully memorized by generations of Cherokee worshipers. Each song is sung in a call-and-response style, with the leader singing a line and those following behind answering with the appropriate words.

The dancing continues late into the night, with even very old people dancing until nearly dawn. At some point during the ceremony, the dancing pauses, and everyone returns to their seats for a sermon. After the Chief has addressed the congregation, an offering is called for, and people line up to deposit money into the offering box located at one of the arbors.

As dawn nears, the group breaks up and people say good-bye. Some will see each other at other stomp grounds that same month. The few remaining stomp grounds have scheduled their dances so that each month there is a dance somewhere every Saturday. Most people, however, have one stomp ground they consider to be "theirs," just as people might be members of a particular church.

In addition to the stomp dance, there are also seven major festivals of the Keetoowah faith. Most stomp grounds still celebrate some or all of

Wampum belts have spiritual significance in traditional Cherokee religion. This display at the Cherokee Cultural Center calls to mind the traditional wampum belts—but each bead in this immense belt stands for a life lost on the Trail of Tears.

these. Perhaps the most important is *Selutsunigististi*, the Green Corn Festi-val, which is celebrated in June or July. Traditional weddings are occasion-ally held as well, and these also take place at the stomp ground.

The proportion of Cherokee who routinely attend the stomp dances or other religious festivals is relatively small, perhaps only 10 percent. This is not entirely because so few people share these beliefs. Many Cherokee live far from the main areas of the tribe and have no chance to attend a stomp ground. Some maintain the old beliefs but feel that these concepts are ade-quately expressed in a Christian church.

Faith in traditional medicine is widespread, even among those who would not consider themselves particularly traditional. While a community might have a few people who are officially known as medicine men, most elders know a little medicine, and people are glad to apply it in their daily lives—for health, peace, or luck. Some have unwavering faith in its abili-ties; others, like one Cherokee teenager at a recent stomp dance, have this attitude: "Whether it works or not, it can't hurt, right?"

While the traditional religious practices of the Cherokee have certainly

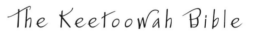

The Keetoowah Bible

Unlike many religions, the "bible" of the Keetoowah faith is not a book. Instead it is depicted as a series of images on seven ancient wampum belts. The belts are made of shells, pearls, and seaweed fibers, and are displayed only on very special occasions.

It is said that originally there was only one large belt. But many years ago, as the tribe prepared for war against another tribe, the medicine men foresaw the outcome of the battle and cut the belt into seven pieces, giving each to a warrior they knew would survive the battle. After the war, the seven belts were scattered, and some were hidden and lost for many years. Redbird Smith recovered the last of the seven belts only eighty years ago.

Some Christian Cherokee worship at New Hope Church.

changed somewhat with the times, it seems to be alive and well, having learned to coexist with the Christian faith and the struggles of the modern world. The songs and dances are being learned by the children and repeated by the adults, guaranteeing that another generation will remember these important pieces of their culture.

Cherokee children inherit their mothers' clan identity.

Chapter 5

Social Structures Today

Although many Cherokee traditions have been well maintained over the years, the basic social structures of the traditional society have broken down. There are many reasons for this; some are the intentional results of government policies, others merely unfortunate consequences of living in a multicultural modern world. Although Cherokee language, arts, and religion continue to thrive, the social structures of most Cherokee are no different than that of the average American.

"Most other tribes consider Cherokees to be very assimilated, perhaps the most assimilated tribe," says Billy Taylor, principal of Kenwood Elementary, a mostly Cherokee school in eastern Oklahoma. "Many consider us more like non-Indians than Indians."

Part of the reason for this can be traced back to some of the earliest contacts with Europeans. The willingness to adopt aspects of other cultures into their own and to coexist with the settlers led to an inevitable weaken-

The Cultural Resource Center helps preserve the traditional heritage that undergirds the Cherokee's social structure.

ing of the basic town and clan structures. The forced resettling during the era of Indian Removals served only to worsen this situation. The concept of individual land ownership ran counter to the Cherokee notion that the people held land in common as a community, and the resulting frictions strained the bonds of tribe and family.

Traditionally, the basic social unit was the village, and every Cherokee village was composed of the same seven clans, each with its own role in village life, including specific religious or political functions. They had their own arbors at the stomp ground, and their own place in the council house. Members of the same clan were considered siblings, and marriage within the clan was forbidden. Children inherited their mothers' clan identity at birth, and their father remained part of his mother's clan.

Clans provided a number of important social functions, such as caring for orphans and the poor, providing for visiting clan members from other villages, and a brutal sort of justice through the law of blood revenge for wrongs committed against clan members; this last function was abolished by the Cherokee Nation government in 1808. The clan also provided each tribe member with a specific place in society.

Unfortunately, the clan structure is essentially gone today. Only a handful of Cherokee still know their clan identity, and even then, the clan has long since ceased to function as it once did. Few records exist as to clan memberships, so most Cherokee will never know their clan.

Intermarriage with settlers began the erosion of the clan structure by imposing the European idea of a male head of family on the *matrilineal* Cherokee society. This breakdown continued as the move to Oklahoma tore apart families and villages. But another large decline in clan affiliation took place in the era following World War II, as Cherokees were scattered across the country, away from their traditional communities.

Large numbers of Cherokee served in the military, and when the war ended many chose to settle elsewhere rather than return to their communities, taking advantage of the skills they had acquired during service or programs like the *GI Bill*. Though some of these Cherokee and their families did eventually return, many more did not, and these Cherokee found themselves out of contact with the old clan structures, even when they did manage to find other Cherokee. Their children grew up without clan affiliation as an important concept in their lives. In many cases, the clan identity was lost entirely.

Beginning in the 1950s, Cherokee began to leave their traditional com-

Today's Cherokee women still gather together for talk and sewing.

This Christmas tree at the Cherokee Cultural Center demonstrates the blending of Cherokee and European social events.

munities for another reason. The federal government established programs to encourage Indians living on tribal land to move to urban areas, and many did so. The stated reason for the programs was to provide Native Americans greater economic opportunities, but although there was probably some truth to this, many Indians merely traded rural poverty for urban poverty. Some suspect that the real motivation was an attempt by the government to break down tribal structures and relieve itself of treaty obligations. Whatever the intent, the economic success of the program was doubtful at best, and the government did away with most of the plan in the 1970s, although many Indians continue to migrate to urban areas in search of jobs and education.

As a result of these programs, large numbers of Cherokee ended up living in cities like Los Angeles and Chicago. While many Cherokee have defied the expectations of *sociologists* and retained their tribal and native identities, the urban environment was fundamentally different from that of the traditional village, and the communities formed in these cities lacked the usual structures. Still, strong communities in American cities have given the urban Cherokee the opportunity to remain in contact with their culture and have helped many new arrivals to feel more at home in the city environment.

Today, most of the responsibilities for social welfare that once rested with the clans now belong to federal and local governments, as they do for most Americans. The tribal governments also play a role in meeting the specific needs of the Cherokee people, in a way playing the role of large "villages" themselves. There are three federally recognized Cherokee tribal governments, two in Oklahoma and one in North Carolina. In addition, while not accorded the legal rights and privileges of an official tribal government, the unofficial bands of Cherokee around the country do provide structure and support for Cherokees in those areas.

Within these official and unofficial groups of Cherokee many smaller communities also exist. For those who belong to these groups, these social bonds are often most important. Scattered throughout the countryside in rural eastern Oklahoma, for example, are many small towns with populations almost completely Cherokee—towns like Kenwood and Chewey, with populations of only a few hundred or less.

In a way, these communities are examples of many of the flaws the

At the Kenwood School in Oklahoma, children learn about their cultural heritage.

North Eastern State University provides Cherokee education to today's young adults.

Cherokee Clans

There are seven different Cherokee clans, although some claim there were once more, even as many as twenty. However many there once were, by the time Europeans visited the Cherokees, each village was comprised of the same seven, though tales persisted of some of the others, like the Ani-Kutani mentioned in chapter two. Each had its own color, traditions, and responsibilities.

Name	Translation	Color
Ani-Wahya	Wolf Clan	Red
Ani-Sahoni	Blue Clan	Blue
Ani-Gilohi	Long Hair Clan	Yellow
Ani-Tsisqua	Bird Clan	Purple
Ani-Wodi	Paint Clan	White
Ani-Kawi	Deer Clan	Brown
Anin-Gatogewi	Wild Potato Clan	Green

government once encouraged Indians to escape. They are isolated and often poor, with few economic opportunities. And yet, despite this, they endure. Many who leave find they eventually return. In these small eastern Oklahoma towns, Cherokee commute several hours to jobs in factories and processing plants in northwest Arkansas or Tulsa; they prefer the long ride to work to leaving the community. "To be tribal," says Billy Taylor, "you need to be part of a community. They have that here."

It is here in these communities that things that were once "normal" for all Cherokee are still the standard, and for many, this is a great a comfort. Rather than their traditions being something that makes them different from those around them, as they are for so many Cherokee in urban areas, here they have something in common, something that binds them together.

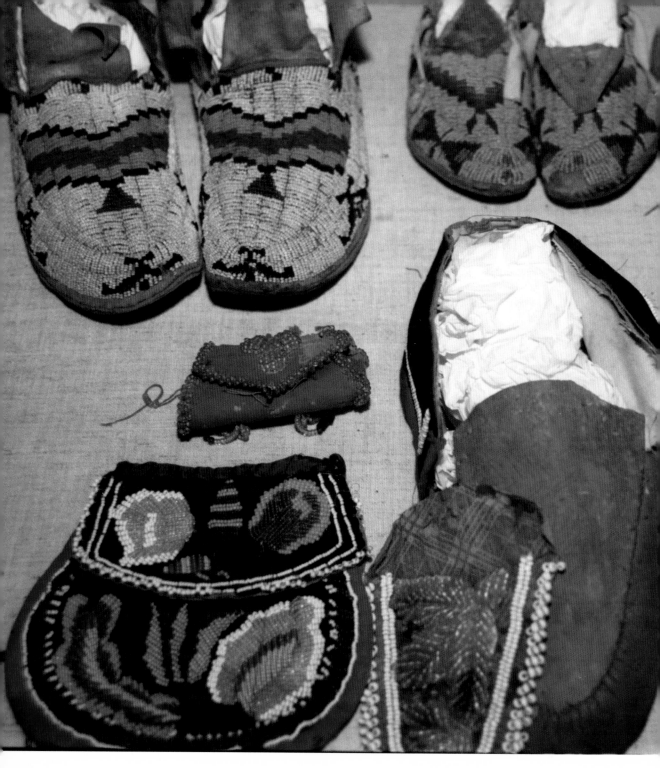

Beadwork reveals the skill and artistry of Cherokee craftspeople.

Chapter 6

Arts and Culture

Like so many aspects of Cherokee life, the arts both preserve the old ways and adapt to new ways. Some crafts, such as pottery and basketry, spring from the practical needs of an ancient people, or from their emotional needs, like ritual or recreation. Others, such as quilting, various forms of painting, and the clothing adapted from European styles, are more recent introductions. The performance arts, both ancient and modern, are also alive and well among the Cherokee. In all these art forms, no matter the style, accomplished Cherokee artists capture a little bit of what it means to be Cherokee.

Cherokee basketry dates back to the earliest days of the tribe, and despite the complex skills involved, it continues to thrive. Before the introduction of metal, glass, and plastic, woven baskets were the main storage container, common items in the ancient Cherokee home. Only women made the baskets, but everyone used them. Baskets stored food and materials, ritual items and tools. Men stored the implements needed for hunting and fishing in them, sometimes using the baskets as packs, and women used some baskets as strainers.

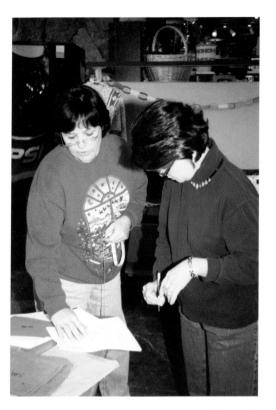

Cherokee women work together to continue traditional fabric arts.

The most distinctly Cherokee of the many types of baskets is the "double-wall" variety, in which the weaver, after working her way to the rim of the basket, doubles back and continues to weave back down the outside. The result is a durable and attractive container. Weavers use reed from strips of cane, oak, honeysuckle, and hickory bark, some of which are dyed with a selection of natural plant dyes. By incorporating strips dyed with different colors, as well as undyed material, the artist creates a design on the basket, generally an abstract pattern. In the past, each clan had its own particular patterns.

In addition to the double-wall basket, flat-weave storage baskets are also a traditional form of basketry. Both these types of baskets are still made today, but while baskets were mostly practical objects in the past, many of today's baskets are intricate works of art with detailed patterns in many colors.

Basketry has always been precise, time-consuming work, but modern basket weavers have taken this to a new level, creating containers that require hundreds of hours of precise planning and construction. Peggy Sanders Brennan, a registered Cherokee from Edmond, Oklahoma, is recognized as one of the finest Native American basket weavers, and her work has been widely praised and displayed. She heads a group of basket weavers called the Oklahoma Native American Basketweavers, who gather to share techniques and preserve the traditions of the Oklahoma tribes.

Another ancient craft is pottery. A few modern potters still make traditional Cherokee pottery, although there seem to be fewer potters than there are basket weavers, and not all modern-day Cherokee potters use entirely traditional processes. Historically, pots were mostly used for cooking and storing liquids, but some designs were used to store seeds or to fill ritual roles. Now, like the baskets, their purpose is mostly decorative.

To make pots, naturally occurring clays are spread, allowed to dry, and then ground between two stones into a fine powder. Impurities are sifted from this powder, and then the clay is rewet until it has absorbed as much water as possible. Using the hands or a wooden paddle, the clay is worked

Sewing machines make fabric work go more quickly for today's Cherokee women.

Arts and Culture 67

A traditional Cherokee dress.

until it reaches the right consistency. In some cases, small amounts of sand or clay are added to make particularly slimy clay stick together better.

When the clay has reached the desired consistency, the potter shapes it into long ropes, which are then wrapped in a coil to form the walls of the pot. Care is taken to make sure no gaps are formed between the layers of rope. When the basic form of the pot has been built, the sides are worked with a stick or stone until the surfaces are tough and smooth. At this point, designs can be added, using either a sharpened stick or a paddle.

When the pot is finally shaped and decorated, it will be allowed to dry for several days before it is fired. A number of methods were traditionally used for firing pots, but the most common included burning ground corncobs or bark inside the pot while firing; this helped to ensure that the pot would be waterproof.

Interest in Cherokee clothing remains strong in the twenty-first century. Although few today wear traditional clothing on a daily basis, many own an outfit or two that they wear for special occasions, like a stomp dance, or a full set of *regalia* for *powwows* or ceremonies. While the ornate dance regalia can be traced back before European contact, most of what is referred to as "traditional" Cherokee clothing is much more modern in nature.

Early Cherokee wore deerskin leggings and dresses; what is today referred to as traditional clothing was heavily influenced by fashions in white

---

Cherokee Basket Dyes

Cherokee dyes were mostly made by soaking various plants in boiling water for about ten minutes, which allowed colored compounds to leach out into the water. Strips to be used for basket weaving would then be placed in the liquid and allowed to soak in the coloring. Generally, the longer the strips are allowed to soak in the liquid, the deeper and more vivid the color.

Below are listed some of the plants used to color Cherokee basketry and the colors they produce.

Plant	Color
Bloodroot	Orange
Walnut Hulls	Various shades of brown
Yellow onion skins	Yellow to rust
Pokeberry	Dark mauve
Butternut	Black
Broom Sedge	Brown
Other berries	Range from reddish to almost black

A Cherokee woman displays a beaded slipper.

society around the time of the Indian Removals. Once again, the Cherokee took ideas from outside their culture and made them their own.

Women wear "tear dresses," so called because they were designed so the material could be torn rather than cut, as few on the Trail of Tears were able to bring scissors. The dresses were about calf length, with buttons up the front of the bodice to allow nursing (very young girls' dresses sometimes fastened up the back), and three-quarter length sleeves, which were long enough to shield the arms from cold or the sun, but short enough to stay out of the way when washing dishes or clothes or doing other manual work. The material was usually cotton *calico* in dark colors or small print, which would resist showing the dirt of daily wear. The Cherokee decorated the dresses with ribbons or solid strips of cotton with cutout designs. Among the Western Cherokee, diamond-shaped designs, representing the mountains of their eastern homeland, are common. Other traditional designs include circles or the seven-point star considered sacred by the Cherokee. Dresses were sometimes made in wool for winter work, and satin or velvet for formal occasions.

Men, too, adapted European-style clothing to fit Cherokee life. While some still wear the turban and jacket for special occasions (made famous by Sequoyah), by far the most common piece of male Cherokee clothing is the ribbon shirt. Patterned after a standard shirt common in the 1800s, it is made in a similar way to the tear dress, usually with narrower decorative ribbons and sometimes with a different colored yoke around the neck and shoulders. The shirt is generally worn untucked. Unlike the tear dress, which has remained largely a Cherokee phenomenon, the ribbon shirt has become commonplace within a number of other tribes, particularly at powwows.

The Cherokee also have a great interest in beadwork, which often decorates moccasins, bags, or dance regalia. It can range from a single line of beads to complex designs requiring tens of thousands of beads—not to mention sharp eyes, a steady hand, and much patience. Many beadwork artists, such as Martha Berry, a registered Cherokee who lives in Texas, tend to combine Cherokee styles with those of other tribes and ideas of their own. The result can be breathtaking.

The Cherokee took quickly to quilting, which provided warmth in the chilly Appalachian highlands and was a good use for fabric scraps. Once again, they developed their own styles, and among the hundreds of classic quilt square patterns known by quilters around the world, many are Cherokee designs. In traditional communities, *quilting bees* are popular events among some women.

Painting is perhaps the most common of all modern-day Cherokee art forms. Native American themes are common. One of the best-loved Cherokee artists is Talmadge Davis, sometimes simply known as Talmadge. A native of Oklahoma, he paints exclusively Cherokee themes: "Our customs and spirituality are hard for the general public to understand, so I try to create a starting point," he says. His work covers the entire span of Cherokee history, from ancient warriors, to the colonial era, to Cherokee veterans of modern wars. He hopes his paintings capture something to which people can relate, allowing them to expand their understanding of Cherokee history.

Another important painter is Dorothy Sullivan. Her paintings often depict women among the early Cherokee, combining elements of realism

In 2002, the University of North Carolina at Chapel Hill introduced a program called the Cherokee Pottery Revitalization Project, led by Brett Riggs. Its goal is to reintroduce through a series of workshops traditional styles to contemporary Cherokee potters among the Eastern Band. The potters approached the archaeology labs at the university about putting together such a program in an effort to preserve an endangered aspect of their heritage and the program has been met with great enthusiasm from the community.

within a layer of spiritual *abstraction*. She has also built a reputation as a portrait painter—of people and horses—and as a commercial artist and draftsperson. She has received many awards, including recognition as the Honored One and Master Artist of the Red Earth Festival in 1999. "My life experiences combined with a growing knowledge of Cherokee history, culture, and legends has given my art purpose—to help preserve my tribal heritage," she says. She fondly recalls listening to her father relate his stories of growing up Cherokee in eastern Oklahoma.

Virginia Stroud is another well-known Cherokee artist. Although Cherokee by birth, she was orphaned at the age of eleven and later adopted into a Kiowa family. A former Miss Indian America, she paints scenes of Native American women in a cheerful, almost cartoonish, style. While not realistic in form, the simple, pleasing pictures sometimes capture a very real sense of emotion in the round-faced figures she depicts.

Less well known perhaps, but no less important, are the craftsmen who make toys. A few Cherokee still make traditional cornhusk dolls, and Cherokee Nation Deputy Principal Chief Hastings Shade recently posted discussion of traditional Cherokee marble making on the tribe's Web site.

The traditional music of the Cherokee stands out among the music of other tribes, being more melodic than the chants of many of their neighbors. Unfortunately, many of the old songs have been lost. Like the tear dress and the ribbon shirt, the "traditional" Cherokee music, with the exception of some of that sung in religious rituals like the stomp dance, is really an adaptation of European styles. Many Christian hymns have been translated into Cherokee, and many newer songs have been written as well. The Cherokee Choir, composed of children, has traveled extensively, performing Cherokee songs and dance. Several musicians have recorded CDs in Cherokee, and the Cherokee Nation recently release a CD of children's songs in Cherokee, featuring adaptations of classic songs ("I'm a Little Terrapin," for example, instead of "I'm a Little Teapot").

Our Fires Still Burn, *a traditional bandolier bag created by Cherokee beadwork artist Martha Berry. Made of wool, cotton, glass beads, and silk, the bag pays tribute to Little Water Spider, the creature who brought the gift of fire to the Cherokee.*

Probably the biggest event in the performing arts for the Cherokee of Oklahoma is the annual Trail of Tears drama. Held in a large outdoor amphitheater near the Cherokee Heritage Center in Tahlequah, the drama runs three days a week from the end of June until Labor Day. It is an enormous production, with a cast of more than 130, that tells the tragic story of the Trail of Tears through dance and vocal performances that have won it a nationwide reputation. The play employs hundreds of people, from set designers and stage crew to the women who sew the hundreds of traditional costumes.

Many Cherokee see the arts as an important means to celebrate their heritage while teaching others, both Indian and non-Indian, about their culture. Some Cherokee practice traditional crafts, while other art is decidedly modern. Either way, their art expresses the world of today's Cherokee.

A statue of Sequoyah reminds visitors to the Cherokee Cultural Center of his gift to the Cherokee people.

Chapter 7

Contributions to the World

In 1958, Mary Ross, great-great-granddaughter of the famous Cherokee chief John Ross, stumped the panel on the popular game show *What's My Line?* Try as they might, not one panelist could guess the occupation of the Cherokee woman, who was already a groundbreaking figure in her field by that time and poised to contribute to some of humanity's greatest triumphs.

No one suspected the truth: Mary Ross was an aerospace engineer, one of the very first women to work in the area. Working as one of the first forty employees of Lockheed Missile and Space Company (now Lockheed-Martin), she had already been involved in the design of the P-28 and Constellation combat aircraft and the Polaris missile. But perhaps her greatest contribution was yet to come. Starting in the late 1950s and continuing into the 1960s, Ross was a critical figure in the development of space flight, contributing significantly to the Agena series of rockets that would play a pivotal role in the Apollo moon missions. She went on to work on a

Admiral Jocko Clark was just one of the many Cherokee who served in the U.S. armed forces.

wide range of space missions, including probes to Mars and Venus and the outer planets.

Ross is not alone among the Cherokee in her contributions to science. Another descendant of John Ross, Robbie Hood, is an atmospheric scientist and hurricane researcher at NASA's Marshall Space Center. Janalee Caldwell and her husband Laurie Vitt, of the Oklahoma Museum of Natural History, study the ecology of the frogs and reptiles of the Amazon rain forest.

But the Cherokee have excelled in more than just scientific research. They are also writers and musicians, actors and honored soldiers. They have served in government on both the local and national level. This chapter cannot hope to name all the Cherokee who have made valuable contributions, but hopefully it will provide an idea of the broad spectrum of fields in which Cherokees have had an impact.

Louis Ballard, recipient of a 2002 Cherokee Medal of Honor Award, is a noted pianist and composer of classical music. Some of his most popular works include *Scenes from Indian Life, Incident at Wounded Knee, The Thunder-beings,* and *Why the Duck Has a Short Tail,* all of which were inspired by his Native American heritage. In addition to writing and performing music, he has also been active in collecting traditional Indian songs and has even put together classroom materials for teaching students about native music.

One of the best-known Cherokee writers is Marilou Awiakta. Born in Knoxville, Tennessee, in 1936, by the time she was in her late thirties she had published more than 1,700 articles and poems. Many of her essays explore the roles of Cherokee women in the atomic age, and she has been praised for promoting *feminist* and Indian perspectives in literature, and for integrating science and the humanities into her work.

By inventing an alphabet for his people, Sequoyah made a great contribution, both to the Cherokee and the world. A written language ensures that a culture's wisdom will endure.

Congressman Brad Carson is a Cherokee who represents the second district of Oklahoma.

Rayna Green is currently the curator of the American Indian Program at the Smithsonian's Museum of American History, but before that she had a long history as a writer and a poet. Her work often focused on the struggles Native American women face in a culture dominated by white men. Her writings frequently urge Indian women to reclaim the honored position they once held in the Cherokee matrilineal society.

Many well-known entertainers claim at least some degree of Cherokee ancestry. Some of these claims are dubious at best. Country great Johnny Cash admitted fabricating the much-repeated story of his Cherokee heritage. Elvis was probably part Cherokee, and there is evidence Jimi Hendrix was as well, but the claims of Cherokee ancestry by many other singers and actors have proven difficult to verify.

Among the best-known entertainers of confirmed Cherokee heritage is actor James Earl Jones, though few are aware of his Indian roots. Although he has appeared in more than 150 movies and TV shows, he did not appear on screen in what is perhaps his most famous role, the voice of Darth

Vader in the original *Star Wars* movies. He also narrated *Black Indians: An American Story*, a documentary that explores issues facing those of mixed Native and African heritage, like himself.

Another well-known performer of mixed Cherokee and African-American background is Della Reese, who is probably best known for her role as Tess on the television program *Touched by an Angel*. In addition to acting, she is also a talented vocalist, having been nominated for a Grammy award as Best Female Soloist in Gospel Music in 1987.

Daughter of a Cherokee mother and Armenian father, singer Cher has had hit singles in several decades, and in 1999, at the age of 52, she became the oldest American woman ever to record a number one hit with her song "Believe." In addition to her music, she is also an accomplished actress and has even directed for television. But no, "Cher" is not short for "Cherokee"—it's from her given name, Cherilyn Sarkisian LaPierre.

Other Cherokee have played more serious roles in society. Some, like Congressman Brad Carson who represents the second district of Oklahoma in Washington, have served in our nation's government. Many others have been elected at the state level, in Oklahoma and elsewhere. The Cherokee FireDancers are a group renowned for their skills in fighting forest fires; they battle blazes in the wilderness all over the United States. They also assisted in the search for debris following the loss of the space shuttle *Columbia*.

Cherokees in Congress

Brad Carson is not the first Cherokee to be elected to Congress. Four other men have preceded him, one in the Senate and three in the House of Representatives:

Robert L. Owens	Senate, Oklahoma	1907–1925
W. W. Hastings	House of Representatives, Oklahoma	1915–1921, 1923–35
Will Rogers, Jr.	House of Representatives, California	1943–1944
Clem Rogers McSpadden	House of Representatives, Oklahoma	1972–1975
Brad Carson	House of Representatives, Oklahoma	2001–

Willa Hebb, a Cherokee, belongs to the Appalachian American Indians of West Virginia, a group dedicated to preserving Native culture for the future.

Cherokee have contributed to our world in one field in particular—the military. Military service is a long and proud tradition among the Cherokee, a continuation of their age-old roles as warriors defending their homeland. Many have served in each of America's wars since the War of 1812, when many Cherokee—including Sequoyah—fought alongside General Andrew Jackson. (As president, Jackson would later drive them from their homeland.) Cherokees fought on both sides of the Civil War, and one, Stand Waite, rose to the rank of Brigadier General in the Confederate Army. In 1866, the U.S. Army established its Indian Scouts unit, which was active throughout the American West and played a role in General John Pershing's pursuit of Mexican bandit Pancho Villa in 1916.

Although the Navajo made "code talkers" famous in World War II, other Indian tribes, including several Cherokee, played a similar role in World

War I. Hundreds, however, were regular soldiers in both World Wars, and many gave their lives on the battlefield in places like Normandy and the Pacific Islands. Their service continued in Korea and Vietnam. Billy Walkabout, a full-blood Cherokee and the most decorated Native American in the Vietnam conflict, received the Distinguished Service Cross for his brave actions in saving the lives of several wounded soldiers in his patrol. Today, many Cherokee serve in all branches of the military and are stationed in the Middle East, Afghanistan, and other places around the world.

In all aspects of life, from science to the arts to national service, Cherokee have made their mark on the United States and the world. No doubt they will continue to do so for years to come.

Powwows are opportunities for Cherokee and other Native groups to share their culture with people across North America. This Cherokee girl at the National Powwow in Washington, D.C., enjoys experimenting with face paint.

As the Cherokee Nation faces a new century, they are rooted in the traditions and history of their past.

Chapter 8

The Future

Most would agree that the Cherokee have come a long way since the devastating losses of the Trail of Tears and the disgrace and humiliation of the "Chief for a Day" era. Despite challenges, they have battled back and remain a proud, vigorous people. That said, it must also be acknowledged that there is much left to be done.

In 1880, Senator Henry Dawes recorded that there was not a single pauper among the Cherokee; by the 1970s, a majority of the Cherokee population in eastern Oklahoma was living below the federal *poverty level*. While this situation has improved somewhat, in the most heavily Cherokee counties in Oklahoma in 2000, roughly 30 percent of the population was still living in poverty. The Cherokee Nation has worked to address this issue and claims progress is being made.

Programs provide assistance with food and heat for poor families, and a special program is set up to address the needs of the elderly, who make up a large proportion of those below the poverty line. Tribal initiatives work to provide day care, so parents can work outside the house. But most of these programs simply treat the symptoms of poverty. The real solution, according to many tribe members, is education.

A program called the "Tribal Work Experience Program" provides work experiences and training opportunities for unemployed heads of households. Dedicated educators in both public and tribal schools work hard to provide Cherokee children with a basic education. Scholarship programs encourage them to go on to college.

However, there are challenges as well. Many states find themselves in the midst of budget crises, and education is often among the sectors hardest hit. At the time of this writing, Oklahoma faces a tremendous budget shortfall. "Sometimes we have plenty of money, but not much flexibility," says Billy Taylor. The school where he teaches in Kenwood, Oklahoma, has one of the best technology systems in Oklahoma, but sometimes struggles to afford basic services.

Comparatively low proportions of Cherokee students go on to college, though this number is growing and owes more to the poverty of many families than to a lack of interest or ability. Most who do go on to higher education are the first in their families to attend college, and many return home to their communities to teach or work.

Overall, Taylor feels his school is headed in the right direction. "It's always going to be a struggle," he says. "People are busy, but there's a lot of

Billy Taylor touches the future when he works with students at Kenwood School.

Cherokee Speakers Today

Research suggests about half of the three languages spoken in North America at the time of Columbus's arrival are now completely extinct, more than half of those within the last seventy-five years. Current estimates of the number of Cherokee speakers are about ten thousand fluent, and not quite half of these read the language. Another twenty thousand know a few words. The majority of speakers are over forty years old. Without intervention, studies indicate the language would be only two generations from extinction, according to the Cherokee Cultural Center's Lisa Stopp. "It's a race against time," says Director Inee Slaughter of the Indigenous Language Institute in Santa Fe, New Mexico.

interest." He points to the 80 to 90 percent of his students who finish high school, a considerable improvement over past years. And he finds it gratifying to work in a school composed almost entirely of Cherokee kids. "Compared to an average school, it's all the same plus more."

In addition to teaching basic skills, teachers at Kenwood often incorporate elements of Cherokee culture into their lessons. Teacher Jan Ballou leads the Cherokee Choir, composed of sixth through ninth grade children from local communities who sing songs ranging from ancient songs to hymns, to country tunes in Cherokee.

One of the biggest emphases today is language education. The Cherokee language has experienced a *renaissance* of sorts, with increased interest and support from both the tribal and federal governments in language instruction. For years the federal government discouraged Indian language instruction, either to ease the Indians' *integration* into the rest of American society or in an attempt to break down tribal identities. Many Cherokee themselves believed that the best thing for the children was to learn English and not Cherokee. Admittedly, a child who spoke no English would be at a disadvantage, even in the Cherokee territory these days, but as a result of such policies, many Cherokee today speak only English.

This loss of their language represents more than simply the loss of

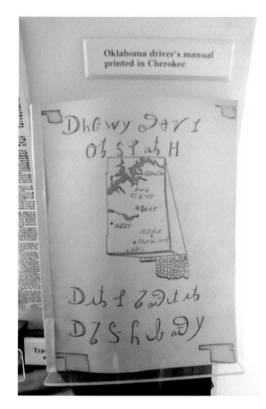

A driver's manual written in the Cherokee language.

another way of saying things. In many ways, it makes it much more difficult to preserve other aspects of the culture. Religious customs and traditional stories all have aspects that are difficult to express outside of the Cherokee tongue.

Because of this, one of the greatest triumphs of the modern Cherokee is the recent increase in language instruction. Many schools in Cherokee communities now have extensive programs of language instruction, and the tribe sponsors programs for both young children and adult learners. The tribe hosts an *immersion* classroom for three- and four-year-olds, and their Web site has on-line lessons and a word list with over seven thousand entries.

Still, in many ways, maintaining the Cherokee tongue remains an uphill battle. Children often see no practical value to the language, and the policies of the past have resulted in a shortage of adult speakers. At Kenwood Elementary, only four teachers out of twelve are fluent in the Cherokee language—but this is more than any other school in the state.

Getting young children interested in learning Cherokee is one of the hardest battles, particularly among those who do not live in Cherokee communities. Lisa LaRue Stopp, of the Cherokee Cultural Center, recalls why one boy changed his mind after an initial disinterest. "I want to be able to talk to my grandma," he said. This is another reason why it is important to preserve the language. In many cases, the Cherokee tongue is the only bridge available to the knowledge of the eldest members of the tribe, who have valuable memories and stories of the past that might otherwise be lost.

Language helps keep a culture alive—and so do the arts. Many Cherokee arts and crafts are flourishing. Cherokee quilters are active, and despite the loss of some of the most noted elder craftspeople, basketry is still going strong. Groups like the Cherokee Choir are helping to keep the tribe's

Teaching the Cherokee language to a new generation is important to maintaining the cultural heritage.

The Cherokee language is used on public signs.

Casinos play an important role in the economic future of the Cherokee Nation.

The Cherokee Cultural Center in Talequah, Oklahoma, reminds the Cherokee of their past as they move into the twenty-first century.

extensive musical history alive as well. Most people seem to value these things, and many show interest in helping to preserve them.

The most basic problem still lies where it has always lain, in the friction and misunderstanding caused by the contact between two cultures. The society of the average American is something a Cherokee needs to understand because it is a reality with which they have to live. But they must be able to do this without losing touch with their own culture. Similarly, non-Indian Americans need to understand Cherokee culture. The challenge lies in teaching both sides to acknowledge the value of both cultures. Non-Indians need to understand the importance of preserving Cherokee culture.

"Too often very mixed blood, assimilated individuals are used to showcase a people," says Lisa Stopp. "It makes it look as though the culture's extinct. The general public looks at mixed bloods, and they say 'See, they're just like us.' But what they need to do is look at recognizable, traditional Indians and be able to say 'See, they're just like us.'"

Despite the trials and tragedy of the past few hundred years, and the challenges facing them in the future, the Cherokee people have survived and thrived, remaining a vibrant, living culture in touch with both the modern world and their ancient past. "The secret of our success," said Wilma Mankiller, a former chief, "is that we never, never give up."

Further Reading

Howard, Greg. *Introduction to Cherokee*. New York: Various Indian Peoples Publishing, 1995.

Kamma, Anne and Connie Roop. *If You Lived with the Cherokee*. New York: Scholastic, 1998.

Mails, Thomas E. *The Cherokee People: The Story of the Cherokee from Earliest Origins to Contemporary Times*. New York: Marlowe, 1996.

Mooney, James. *Myths of the Cherokee*. Mineola, N.Y.: Dover, 1996.

Sturm, Circe. *Blood Politics: Race, Culture, and Identity in the Cherokee Nation of Oklahoma*. Berkeley: University of California Press, 2002.

For More Information

Cherokee Indians
www.smokymtnmall.com/mall/cindians.html

Cherokee Nation
www.cherokee.org

Eastern Band of Cherokees
www.cherokee-nc.com

History of the Cherokee
cherokeehistory.com

North Georgia's Cherokee
ngeorgia.com/history/cherokee.html

Publisher's Note:

The Web sites listed on this page were active at the time of publication. The publisher is not responsible for Web sites that have changed their address or discontinued operation since the date of publication. The publisher will review and update the Web sites upon each reprint.

Glossary

abstraction: Something that cannot be realistically represented or imagined in a concrete form.

activist: Someone who does things in support of a cause.

apprentice: Someone who is learning a trade by working with an experienced person.

archive: A place where public records and historical documents are preserved.

assimilated: Blended into the culture of a population.

autonomous: Having the right to self-government.

bilingual: The ability to communicate in two languages.

calico: Any of various inexpensive cotton fabrics with patterns.

conjurer: Someone who practices magic arts.

constitution: The basic principles and laws of a nation, state, or social organization.

contentious: Likely to cause an argument.

criteria: Standards on which decisions or judgments are made.

diverse: Having different characteristics.

emancipated: Freed from control by another.

exodus: A mass departure.

feminist: Someone who supports the theory of the political, economic, and social equality of the sexes.

fry bread: A quick bread cooked by deep-frying.

GI Bill: A federal program begun in 1944 of educational and other benefits for returning servicemen.

immersion: A sudden plunge into something.

innovations: New ideas or methods.

integration: To incorporate into a society or organization people of different groups (races).

intricacies: Complicated workings.

marginalized: Made outside the mainstream of society.

matrilineal: Tracing descent through the line of the mother.

medicine men: Priestly healers.

migration: Moving from one place to another.

Mount Sinai: Mountain in Egypt where Moses received the Ten Commandments from God.

negotiate: To arrange a compromise through discussion.

neutrality: Refusal to take part in a war between other powers.

poverty level: A government established level of income below which someone is considered poor. Also called poverty line.

powwows: Native American social gatherings highlighting dancing and other cultural demonstrations.

quilting bees: Gatherings of women to work on quilts and socialize.

ratified: Officially approved.

regalia: Special costume.

renaissance: A rebirth; revival.

reservation: A tract of public land put aside for use by Native Americans.

sociologists: People who study the science of society, social institutions, and social relationships.

sovereignty: Freedom from external control.

traditionalists: People who prefer to follow the customs and beliefs of their ancestors.

wards: People under the legal protection of a government or person.

Index

Biographies

Philip Stewart was born in western New York State and raised near the Seneca Indian reservations there, where he developed an early interest in Native American culture. After graduating from nearby Alfred University, he worked for several years at Cornell University, before moving to Fayetteville, Arkansas, to attend graduate school at the University of Arkansas. He lives there with his wife Cynthia and daughter Zea.

Benjamin Stewart, a graduate of Alfred University, is a freelance photographer and graphic artist. He traveled across North America to take the photographs included in this series.

Martha McCollough received her bachelor's and master's degrees in anthropology at the University of Alaska-Fairbanks, and she now teaches at the University of Nebraska. Her areas of study are contemporary Native American issues, ethnohistory, and the political and economic issues that surround encounters between North American Indians and Euroamericans.